Riding on a Bus

by Dorothy Chlad

Illustrations by Lydia Halverson

CHICAGO

Library of Congress Cataloging in Publication Data

Chlad, Dorothy.
　　Riding on a bus.

　　(Safety Town)
　　Summary: A child describes the safety precautions he and his friends take while riding on buses.
　　1. Children's accidents—Prevention—Juvenile literature. 2. Buses—Safety measures—Juvenile literature. 3. Traffic safety and children—Juvenile literature. [1. Buses—Safety measures. 2. Safety]
I. Title. II. Series: Chlad, Dorothy. Safety Town.
HV675.5.C47　1985　　613.6'8　　85-12750
ISBN 0-516-01979-1　　　　AACR2

Copyright ©1985 by Regensteiner Publishing Enterprises, Inc.
All rights reserved. Published simultaneously in Canada.
Printed in the United States of America.
　　3 4 5 6 7 8 9 10 R 94 93 92 91 90 89 88

Hi. My name is Bobby.

Would you like to be a bus driver's helper?

This is how my friends and I help the bus driver.

We wait in line.

When the bus is near, the driver puts on blinking lights.

We wait until the bus stops at the edge of the sidewalk or roadway.

When the driver opens the door, we get on one at a time.

We hold on to the rail.

The bus driver works hard. He watches for cars, motorcycles, bicycles, and walkers.

He also listens for police and ambulance sirens.

My friends and I talk quietly so the driver can hear.

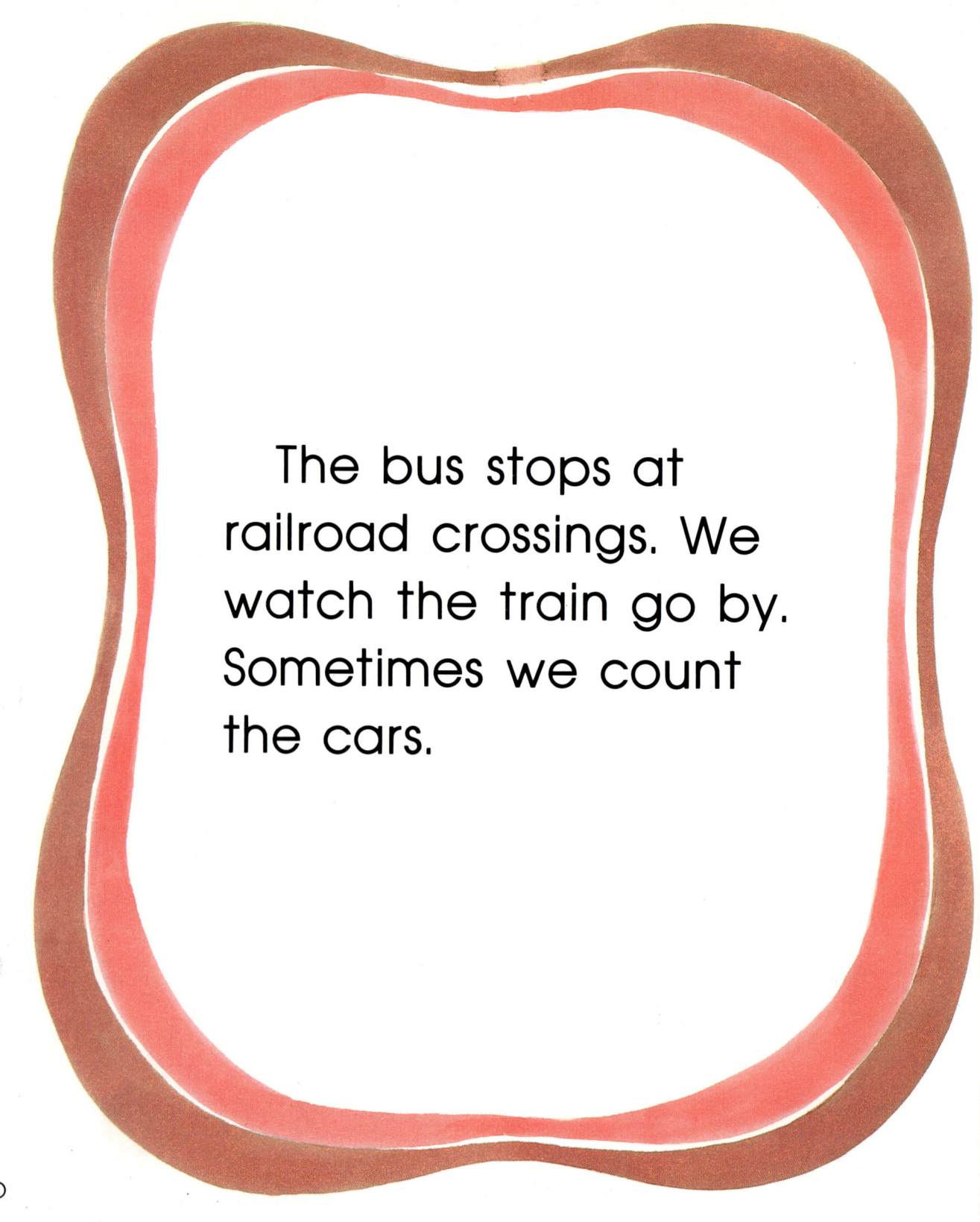

The bus stops at railroad crossings. We watch the train go by. Sometimes we count the cars.

When we get off the bus, we wait our turn.

Sometimes I ride a bus with my mom and dad.

We go shopping.

When we go to
the country, we take
the bus.
We visit Grandma
and Grandpa.

It's fun to ride a bus
any time of year.

You and your friends can be the bus driver's helpers, too.

Remember to:

Wait in line behind the edge of the sidewalk or roadway.

Wait for the bus to come to a stop.

Hold on to the rail.

Sit back in the seat.

Talk in a quiet voice.

About the Author

Dorothy Chlad, founder of the total concept of Safety Town, is recognized internationally as a leader in Preschool/Early Childhood Safety Education. She has authored eight books on the program, and has conducted the only workshops dedicated to the concept. Under Mrs. Chlad's direction, the National Safety Town Center was founded to promote the program through community involvement.

She has presented the importance of safety education at local, state, and national safety and education conferences, such as National Community Education Association, National Safety Council, and the American Driver and Traffic Safety Education Association. She serves as a member of several national committees, such as the Highway Traffic Safety Division and the Educational Resources Division of National Safety Council. Chlad was an active participant at the Sixth International Conference on Safety Education.

Dorothy Chlad continues to serve as a consultant for State Departments of Safety and Education. She has also consulted for the TV program, "Sesame Street" and recently wrote this series of safety books for Childrens Press.

A participant of White House Conferences on safety, Dorothy Chlad has received numerous honors and awards including National Volunteer Activist and YMCA Career Woman of Achievement. In 1983, Dorothy Chlad was one of sixty people nationally to receive the **President's Volunteer Action Award** from President Reagan for twenty years of Safety Town efforts. She has also been selected for inclusion in **Who's Who of American Women**, the **Personalities of America**, the **International Directory of Distinguished Leadership**, **Who's Who of the Midwest**, and the 8th Edition of **The World Who's Who of Women.**

About the Artist

Lydia Halverson was born Lydia Geretti in midtown Manhattan. When she was two, her parents left New York and moved to Italy. Four years later her family returned to the United States and settled in the Chicago Area. Lydia attended the University of Illinois, graduating with a degree in fine arts. She worked as a graphic designer for many years before finally concentrating on book illustration.